D0968454

How to Stop Candida & Other Yeast Conditions *in Their Tracks*

VALERIE SAXION

Strength
& Honor

BRONZE BOW PUBLISHING
www.bronzebowpublishing.com

BOOKS BY VALERIE SAXION

Conquering the Fatigue, Depression, and Weight Gain Caused by Low Thyroid

Every Body Has Parasites

How to Detoxify and Renew Your Body From Within

How to Feel Great All the Time

The Easy Way to Regain and Maintain Your Perfect Weight

How to Stop Candida and Other Yeast Conditions in Their Tracks

Copyright © 2003 Valerie Saxion

All Scripture quotations, unless otherwise indicated, are taken from the *Holy Bible, New International Version®.* NIV®. Copyright © 1973, 1978, 1984 by International Bible Society. Used by permission of Zondervan Publishing House. All rights reserved.

ISBN 0-9724563-7-6

Published by Bronze Bow Publishing, Inc., 2600 East 26th Street, Minneapolis, MN 55406

You can reach us on the internet at www.bronzebowpublishing.com

Literary development and cover/interior design by Koechel Peterson & Associates, Minneapolis, Minnesota.

Manufactured in the United States of America

CONTENTS

ABOUT THE AUTHOR

DR. VALERIE SAXION is one of America's most articulate champions of nutrition and spiritual healing. A twenty-year veteran of health science with a primary focus in Naturopathy, Valerie has a delightful communication style and charming demeanor that will open your heart, clear your mind, and uplift you to discover abundant natural health God's way.

As the co-founder of Valerie Saxion's Silver Creek Labs, a manufacturer and distributor of nutritional supplements and health products, Dr. Saxion has seen firsthand the power of God's remedies as the sick are healed and the lame walk.

Valerie is seen regularly on the weekly Trinity Broadcasting Network program *On Call* that airs worldwide on TBN, Sky Angel, Daystar, and the Health & Healing television networks. She has been interviewed on numerous radio talk shows as well as television appearances. Hosts love to open the line for callers to phone in their health concerns while Dr. Saxion gives on-the-air advice and instruction.

Dr. Saxion has also lectured at scores of health events nationwide and in Canada. After attending one of her lectures, you will leave empowered with the tools to live and love in a healthy body!

To schedule Dr. Saxion for a lecture or interview, please contact Joy at 1-800-493-1146, or fax 817-236-5411, or email at: valeriesaxon@cs.com.

Married to Jim Saxion for twenty-plus years, they are the parents of eight healthy children, ages 1 to 21.

WHAT IS CANDIDA ALBICANS?

FOR HUNDREDS OF YEARS it has been known that a tiny yeast organism (a fungus) called *Candida albicans*, which lives naturally in all healthy bodies, can cause vaginal problems and skin and mouth rashes. Since the time of Hippocrates (400 B.C.), yeast infections have been known as a problem. But never before have they plagued the human race so intensely as they do today. Seven out of ten women get at least one attack of *Candida* overgrowth or thrush in their lives. It is also common for babies to develop this in their diaper area or in their mouths.

But since Dr. C. Orian Truss, an internist and allergist, first reported the relationship of yeast to many of his patients' illnesses in a series of articles in the *Journal of Orthomolecular Psychiatry* in 1978, the word has spread to physicians as well as to those who have suffered from yeast-related health disorders. Thanks to Dr. Truss we now know a host of other symptoms that can be caused by *Candida* overgrowths.

- constipation
- diarrhea
- colitis
- nail fungus
- abdominal pain
- headaches
- bad breath
- rectal itching
- impotence
- memory loss
- mood swings
- prostatitis
- canker sores
- persistent heartburn
- muscle and joint pain
- sore throat
- congestion
- nagging cough
- numbness in the face or extremities
- tingling sensations
- acne
- night sweats
- severe itching
- clogged sinuses
- PMS
- burning tongue
- white spots on the tongue and in the mouth
- vaginitis
- kidney and bladder infections
- arthritis
- depression
- hyperactivity
- hypothyroidism
- adrenal problems
- Jock itch
- athlete's foot
- even diabetes
- immune weakness
- poor digestion
- chronic fatigue
- bloating
- gas
- poor elimination
- sugar and carbohydrate cravings
- head pain
- brain fog
- female issues
- skin rashes
- cold hands or feet

If you suffer from any of these symptoms, there is a chance that it may be yeast-related. From my years of treating *Candida*, I can assure you that it will disguise itself in everything from athlete's foot to low blood sugar to obesity. *Disguise* is the operative word for *Candida*.

Candida albicans is a parasitic yeastlike fungus that exists naturally in the body and usually causes no bad effects. It mainly inhabits the digestive tract but can spread to other parts of the body such as the esophagus, mouth, throat, genital area, and even the lungs in severe cases. In a normal healthy body, these harmless parasites coexist in small colonies along with the other bacteria found in our digestive system.

The immune system and the "friendly" bacteria in our intestines (*Bifidobacteria bifidum* and *Lactobacillus acidophilus*) keep *Candida* overgrowth under control most of the time in a healthy body. These bacteria and others make up the normal bacterial population of our gastrointestinal tract and are often referred to as "GI microflora." They exist in a symbiotic relationship with us and are essential for maintaining healthy intestines and resisting infections. However, when an imbalance occurs in the natural bacterial environment, which can be caused by a variety of factors, then the *Candida albicans* organisms begin to grow at a rapid rate and spread and infect the body tissues.

These "colonies" of the *Candida albicans* are anaerobic organisms (existing in the absence of oxygen), and when they occur in large numbers, they can release their toxic waste directly into the bloodstream, which can cause any of the symptoms noted above. It is estimated that over 90 percent of the U.S. population has some degree of *Candida* overgrowth in their bodies.

THE CAUSES OF CANDIDA ALBICANS

Why does this yeast, which is normally harmless, tend to grow out of control? There are a number of factors that reduce our natural resistance and contribute to *Candidiasis,* an overgrowth of *Candida.* These causes include:

1. Extended use of antibiotics. The prevalence that we now see with the *Candida* problem can be attributed in large part to the widespread use of broad-spectrum antibiotics that are prescribed for all kinds of infections. They are especially harmful because they destroy not only the disease-causing bacteria but also the "friendly"

bacteria that help to control the *Candida* bacteria. As a result, an imbalance occurs in the pH levels of our intestines, which in turn stimulates the growth of the *Candida.* Antibiotics are also found in many foods as residue, resulting from their use in food animals.

The Latin definition of a *biotic* is *life.* So an antibiotic is anti-life, and a probiotic is pro-life.

2. **Oral contraceptives and cortisone-type steroids.** These types of drugs cause a hormone imbalance and weaken the body, which also favors the growth of *Candida.*

3. **Low levels of acidophilus and bifidus bacteria in the colon.** When these "friendly" bacteria levels are reduced, then the *Candida* bacteria have free reign to grow out of control.

4. **Improper diets.** The average American diet is also a cause for *Candida.* A lot of the food we consume is overprocessed, high in refined sugar and carbohydrates, colored, and low in fiber. It is no wonder that we have a problem with yeast infections when you consider all the fast food we eat in our fast paced society. Our lifestyles have drastically affected our eating habits. According to a *Journal of American Medical Association* article in 1977, this kind

of diet results in fewer "friendly" bacteria in our gastrointestinal tract. Those conditions then favor the onset of *Candidiasis*.

5. Chemicals. It is no secret that since the turn of the twentieth century we have introduced thousands of chemicals into our environment. We have paid a price in terms of our health because prolonged exposure to many of them over the years has had a host of adverse effects on our health. A number of those chemicals have entered our food chains through growth hormones given to livestock or by chemicals used in the feed to prevent disease. Other chemicals and pollutants such as fertilizers have leached off thousands of farms into rivers and streams, thus contaminating fish. It is a sad commentary on the state of our environment that in some states information on contaminated streams and rivers is given when fishing licenses are issued. Even chemicals such as chlorine found in our drinking water can have an effect on the growth of *Candida albicans*.

6. Hypothyroidism. It is highly probable that if you have *Candida*, you also have low thyroid, which often goes undiagnosed and untreated. Hypothyroidism slows the body's metabolism

and lowers the body temperature, reducing its effectiveness to kill off bacteria and allowing *Candida* to thrive. It is essential that your thyroid is functioning efficiently and that your body metabolism is running at full capacity if you want to keep your body free of *Candida*.

It can be one of these causes or a combination of all of them to different degrees that can throw our bodies out of balance. The human body was "fearfully and wonderfully made," but it has its limits also. When we cross those limits, and a serious flare-up of *Candidiasis* occurs, then we may experience a variety of alarming symptoms.

THE SYMPTOMS OF CANDIDA ALBICANS

Yeast infections can occur in anybody at any age, but they are more prevalent in women. When our body systems become imbalanced, then a yeast overgrowth can occur. It is possible for someone to have a problem for a while before they manifest symptoms.

Candida albicans can exist in two forms: yeast and fungal. Serious health problems can develop when it changes its anatomy to a fungal form. In that state, the organisms produce rhizoids (very long rootlike structures) that penetrate the mucous lining of the intestines. These rhizoids leave tiny holes that break down the natural barrier between the intestines and the circulatory system and allow toxins, bacteria, yeast, and even small undigested food particles direct access to the bloodstream. Once these toxins enter the bloodstream, they can travel throughout the entire body and produce a number of adverse symptoms that further weaken the immune system. I refer you back to the list of symptoms we outlined previously.

Symptoms often worsen in damp and/or moldy places, and after consumption of foods containing sugar and/or yeast, as well as after a round of antibiotics. Because this disorder is oftentimes misdiagnosed, many individual symptoms are treated, but the sufferer from *Candida albicans* often never gets to the root of the problem.

People who have been battling any chronic symptoms listed above without relief should explore the possibility of *Candida* overgrowth and take the necessary steps to alleviate this condition. The following is one way to determine if you have a problem with *Candida*.

CANDIDA ALBICANS SELF-TEST

IN ORDER TO PROPERLY UNDERSTAND
AND DIAGNOSE whether you have a problem with *Candida albicans*, it is necessary to take a look at your personal medical history and administer a *Candida* questionnaire. The information will then help determine what may have promoted the *Candida* growth in the first place. Circle the points below that apply to you and then add the total at the end of the section.

The following questionnaire was originally designed by Dr. William G. Crook and published in his book, *The Yeast Connection: A Medical Breakthrough*, in 1983. Several years ago a friend passed it along to me as a simple printout without any credits. We made slight modifications to the questionnaire and have been using it effectively with clients for years. It is designed for adults and is not appropriate for children. The original questionnaire is available from Professional Books, P.O. Box 3494, Jackson, Tennessee 38301 (prices on request).

The diagnosis of *Candida albicans* is somewhat controversial, as there is no definitive scientific test to show it as a causative indicator. If your test score is high, and you think you have this problem, you may wish to consult a licensed medical professional. Information in this booklet, including comments on medical treatments, is not intended as medical advice. It should be evaluated critically and should not take the place of medical advice from a licensed healthcare professional.

PERSONAL HISTORY QUESTIONNAIRE

1. During your lifetime, have you taken any antibiotics or tetracyclines (symycin, Panmycin, Vibramycin, Monicin, etc.) for acne or other conditions for more than one month?   25 pts.

2. Have you taken a broad-spectrum antibiotic for more than 2 months or 4 or more times in a 1-year period? These could include any antibiotics taken for respiratory, urinary, or other infections.   20 pts.

3. Have you taken a broad-spectrum antibiotic even for a single course? These antibiotics include ampicillin, amoxicillin, Keflex, etc.   6 pts.
4. Have you ever had problems with persistent Prostatitis, vaginitis, or other problems with your repro-ductive organs?   25 pts.
5. Women—Have you been pregnant?
   2 or more times?   5 pts.
   1 time?   3 pts.
6. Women—Have you taken birth control pills?
   More than 2 years?   15 pts.
   More than 6 months?   8 pts.
7. If you were NOT breast-fed as an infant.   9 pts.
8. Have you taken any cortisone-type drugs (Prednisone, Decadron, etc.)?   15 pts.
9. Are you sensitive to and bothered by exposure to perfumes, insecticides, or other chemical odors . . .   20 pts.
   Do you have moderate to severe symptoms?   20 pts.
   Mild symptoms?   5 pts.
10. Does tobacco smoke bother you?   10 pts.

11. Are your symptoms worse on damp, muggy days or in moldy places? 20 pts.

12. If you have had chronic fungus infections of the skin or nails (including athlete's foot, ring-worm, jock itch), have the infections been . . .
    Severe or persistent? 20 pts.
    Mild to moderate? 10 pts.

13. Do you crave sugar (chocolate, ice cream, candy, cookies, etc.)? 10 pts.

14. Do you crave carbohydrates (bread, bread, and more bread)? 10 pts.

15. Do you crave alcoholic beverages? 10 pts.

16. Have you drunk or do you drink chlorinated water (city or tap)? 20 pts.

TOTAL _____

SCORE YOUR SYMPTOMS

For each of your symptoms, enter the corresponding number in the point score column.

No symptoms 0
Occasional or mild 3
Frequent or moderately severe 6
Severe and/or disabling 9

SYMPTOMS	POINTS
1. Constipation	_____
2. Diarrhea	_____
3. Bloating	_____
4. Fatigue or lethargy	_____
5. Feeling drained	_____
6. Poor memory	_____
7. Difficulty focusing/brain fog	_____
8. Feeling moody or despaired	_____
9. Numbness, burning, or tingling	_____
10. Muscle aches	_____
11. Nasal congestion or discharge	_____
12. Pain and/or swelling in the joints	_____
13. Abdominal pain	_____
14. Spots in front of the eyes	_____
15. Erratic vision	_____
16. Cold hands and/or feet	_____
17. Women—endometriosis	_____
18. Women—menstrual irregularities	_____
19. Women—premenstrual tension	_____
20. Women—vaginal discharge	_____
21. Women—persistent vaginal burning or itching	_____
22. Men—prostatitis	_____
23. Men—impotence	_____
24. Loss of sexual desire	_____

25. Low blood sugar
26. Anger or frustration
27. Dry patchy skin
TOTAL

CANDIDA SELF-TEST

For each of your symptoms, enter the appropriate figure in the point score column.

No symptoms 0
Occasional or mild 3
Frequent or moderately severe 6
Severe and/or disabling 9

1. Heartburn
2. Indigestion
3. Belching and intestinal gas
4. Drowsiness
5. Itching
6. Rashes
7. Irritability or jitters
8. Uncoordinated
9. Inability to concentrate
10. Frequent mood swings
11. Postnasal drip
12. Nasal itching
13. Failing vision

14. Burning or tearing of the eyes _____
15. Recurrent infections or fluid
    in the ears _____
16. Ear pain or deafness _____
17. Headaches _____
18. Dizziness/loss of balance _____
19. Pressure above the ears—your
    head feels as though it is swelling _____
20. Mucus in the stools _____
21. Hemorrhoids _____
22. Dry mouth _____
23. Rash or blisters in the mouth _____
24. Bad breath _____
25. Sore or dry throat _____
26. Cough _____
27. Pain or tightness in the chest _____
28. Wheezing or shortness of breath _____
29. Urinary urgency or frequency _____
30. Burning during urination _____
TOTAL _____

CANDIDA SELF-ANALYSIS RESULTS

Total Score from Section 1
Total Score from Section 2 _____
Total Score from Section 3 _____
TOTAL SCORE _____

If your score is at least: Your symptoms are:
180 Women/140 Men Almost certainly yeast
                                  connected
120 Women/90 Men   Probably yeast
                                  connected
60 Women/40 Men   Possibly yeast
                                  connected

If your score is less than:
60 Women/40 Men   Probably not yeast
                                  connected

If you scored below 60 for women or 40 for men, WAY TO GO! You are probably not plagued with the symptoms of *Candida albicans*. You are obviously following a very healthy lifestyle, and you deserve a huge pat on the back! However, if your score was above 60 for women or 40 for men, you may want to consider looking into a means to get the *Candida* overgrowth under control.

TREATMENT OF CANDIDA ALBICANS

IF YOU ARE GOING TO RID YOUR BODY OF *CANDIDA* SUCCESSFULLY, then you are going to have to make changes in your lifestyle. The most important first step to overcoming this infection will be changing your diet. Yeasts thrive on carbohydrates, especially foods that contain table sugar and refined forms of sucrose, glucose, and fructose. A sugar-free, yeast-free diet is key to bringing the *Candida* in your digestive track back under control. Not only must you starve the yeast, but you must also provide all the essential nutrients needed for the healing process, particularly Niacin and Vitamins A, B, C, and E.

Our goal is to rid the body of the yeast overgrowth and restore the normal flora balance in our intestines so that our body can heal itself. A clean colon is essential if we are going to succeed against a severe case of *Candida albicans*. I personally recommend enemas as an absolute must. Enemas assist the body in its detoxifying effort by cleansing out all the toxic waste from the alimentary canal. A healthy, normal adult is carrying around 7-14 pounds of waste (that's the weight of a new-born baby!). Think of what an immune-compromised or overweight person may have stored up because of their improper diet.

It is extremely important that you remove old impacted fecal matter and excess mucus that is adhering to the inner wall of your intestinal walls. Because *Candida albicans* thrive in environments that are warm, putrid, and lacking in oxygen, it is necessary to thoroughly cleanse your intestines. Enemas should be taken at least once, preferably twice, a day during your time of cleansing—one after rising in the morning and the other before going to bed. One pint to one quart of lukewarm distilled water is sufficient. Enema bags are available in any drugstore. One word of medical caution—enemas tend to delete the potassium level, therefore care must be taken for proper supplementation.

The following are recommendations to rid the body and starve out the *Candida:*

DO'S

■ I offer a new product in tablet form called *Candida Cleanse* that can eliminate the overgrowth as well as help to normalize bowel functions. You'll find more information about it and another product, *ParaCease,* at the back of the book under "Valerie Saxion's Silver Creek Labs."

■ Read "Dealing With Hypothyroidism" in my book, *How to Feel Great All the Time.* If your body metabolism is running slow as a result of low thyroid, your body temperature may also be low, which reduces the body's effectiveness in killing off bad bacteria such as *Candida.* It is highly probable that it is a major factor as relates to *Candida.*

■ Change toothbrushes every 30 days, as mold and fungus will tend to grow over prolonged use. Daily rinse your toothbrush with a good *food grade* hydrogen peroxide to kill bacteria on the brush as well as in the mouth. After rinsing the toothbrush with 3 percent hydrogen peroxide, do not wash off with tap water.

- Pau d'arco tea contains an antibacterial agent and can be used up to six times a day until symptoms subside. It also comes in a tincture (30-40 drops taken in water, 3 times daily) and in capsules (2 capsules, 3 times daily). Alternating with Clove tea is an excellent way to kill the fungus.

- Use only steam-distilled water when cooking. And you should be drinking half your weight in ounces of steam-distilled water to eliminate chemical contaminants. For instance, if you weigh 128 pounds, you should drink 64 ounces or half a gallon spaced throughout the day.

- Eat a cup of oat bran daily to speed up elimination.

- Eat fresh and raw vegetables, which will help to restore the normal intestinal flora in your body. Bake, broil, or steam your vegetables.

- Radishes contain sulfur, selenium, and antibiotics. Onions are antifungal and provide sulfur. Avocados have antifungal fatty acids and are sugar-free.

- If you are suffering with jock itch, clean the area in the morning and evening with

Tea Tree oil. Dilute 8 drops of Tea Tree oil in 8 ounces of warm distilled water and clean with a cloth.

- Ginger root and horseradish have anti-septic enzymes and oils. Oregano and cumin have antifungal essentials oils. Basil contains antifungal volatile oils.
- Eat yogurt (no Aspartame®) daily, as much as possible, with live active cultures that are documented on the label! These help to restore the natural "friendly" bacteria to your gastrointestinal tract.
- Kyolic® garlic (2 capsules, 3 times per day) is very helpful, and a good B-Complex is an excellent addition. Garlic is a natural antibiotic with properties that stimulate the gut flora to work more efficiently.
- Capricin®, (Cayenne pepper) 4 capsules, 3 times per day.
- Natren Probiotics, daily. It creates a good terrain for aerobic bacteria (good bacteria) to live and thrive in, also use,
- *Body Oxygen*™ 2-3 times per day and,
- *Oxygen Bath*™ 2-3 per week.
- Lastly, take a good supplement that attacks the *Candida*.

DON'TS

■ Avoid taking antibiotics unless absolutely necessary. Remember to eat plenty of yogurt if you do take a round of antibiotics that have been prescribed by a physician.

■ Avoid oral contraceptives and cortisone products, which work against the effectiveness of this regime. If you need to take them, please discuss it with your health care professional.

■ Avoid sugar in any form, including fruit, honey, molasses, maple syrup, and all alcoholic beverages, especially white wine.

■ Avoid aged cheeses, chocolate, fermented foods, all grains containing gluten, pork, nut butters, pickles, raw mushrooms, soy sauce, sprouts, vinegar, and all yeast-containing products.

■ Avoid citrus and acid fruits (orange, grapefruit, tomatoes, pineapple, and limes) until all signs of *Candida* are gone for 3 months.

■ Avoid all meats that have been treated with hormones or chemicals.

■ Avoid saturated fats.

TYPICAL CASES OF CANDIDA

CANDIDA OUTGROWTHS ARE TYPICALLY CALLED THRUSH. There are three common symptoms of it, but all are *Candida*-related.

ORAL THRUSH

This is an infection that appears as raised, creamy spots on the mucus membranes lining the mouth, lips, and throat. When rubbed, the spots are sore and red underneath. It occurs in children as well as adults, and in cases of serious immune deficiencies, such as AIDS, oral thrush can spread to the lungs and become life-threatening.

Babies may develop oral thrush as well. From here the infection may be transferred to the mother's nipples, if she is breast-feeding. The symptoms of nipple thrush include redness, soreness, swelling, and cracking that is not soothed by the usual nipple emollient creams.

Oral thrush usually responds quickly to

treatment, and treatment should begin as quickly as possible. The longer the *Candida* overgrows, the harder it is to get rid of. It responds well to various herbal mouthwashes such as tinctures of myrrh or marigold, and also to a mouthwash of Tea Tree oil with oil of myrrh diluted in water three times a day. A gargle of thyme, melissa, and lavendar may help. A traditional doctor will usually treat oral thrush with antifungal drugs (Clotrimazole® or Nystatin®), which are taken orally and swished around in the mouth.

Beyond that, you should utilize the other treatments for *Candida* that I listed previously. Oral thrush is an indication that your entire immune system is weak. Your body needs to be cleansed, sugar-free, and boosted with all the nutrients that promote health. Always . . . always take a probiotic at these times.

VAGINAL THRUSH

Thriving in warm, damp enclosed areas, *Candida* overgrowths often occur in the vagina with painful effects. Symptoms include a discharge that is thick, white, and looks like curd cheese. The vulva may become sore, dry, red, and itchy, and one might experience a stinging sensation during urination. At times a red rash will extend down the thighs or around the anus. And intercourse may be very uncomfortable with vaginal thrush.

Vaginal thrush results from the same five causes of *Candida* that we listed previously, with the added factor of a woman's hormonal change at pregnancy or during the last week of a menstrual cycle. When the vaginal acidity is altered, it makes it easier for *Candida* to flourish. A high intake of sugar and yeast can also set it off by raising the glucose level in all the cells of the body. Thrush can also be aggravated by anything that irritates the delicate vaginal or labial tissues—intercourse, poor hygiene, tight clothing, tampons, scented or bubble bath preparations.

I recommend that you clean the genital area in the morning and evening with Tea Tree oil. Dilute 8 drops of Tea Tree oil in 8 ounces of warm distilled water and clean with a cotton cloth. Douching 2-3 times per week with an H_2O_2 mixture of 1 ounce 3 percent food-grade hydrogen peroxide to 11 ounces distilled water may be helpful. A traditional M.D.

will treat vaginal thrush with antifungal drugs such as Clotrimazole® or Nystatin®, in the form of ointments, creams, or pessaries.

Women with recurring vaginal thrush may spread the infection to their mate. I recommend that their partner employ a treatment simultaneous to theirs. Thrush may affect him without any visible symptoms and may cause reinfection.

As noted with oral thrush, every one of the treatments for *Candida* should be implemented to bring health to your entire system. And do yourself a favor—avoid tight-fitting clothes and wear cotton underwear, which allows for "breathing." Stay away from scented soaps, shower gels, and bath preparations that can stir an attack.

THRUSH THAT ACCOMPANIES DIAPER RASH

In infants, *Candidiasis* can accompany diaper rash. The skin irritation occurs by contact with urine and feces, which weakens the skin's barrier to infection and makes it vulnerable to thrush. It takes the appearance of a red rash with flaky white patches. It may be sore, itchy, or cause little discomfort for some babies.

To treat thrush in the diaper area, a drop of antifungal Tea Tree oil in apricot carrier oil can be smoothed on. There are also antifungal drugs in the form of creams and ointments that can be used.

And here's a tip that will save you the cost of a doctor's visit and an expensive prescription: try Gentian Violet. You'll find it at your pharmacy, and it's effective, fast-acting, and inexpensive. One word of caution: it is violet and will stain other garments, so use carefully.

SPECIFIC SEVERE CASES OF CANDIDA

CASE #1

A MALE ELECTRICIAN (AGE 35-40) CAME IN FOR A CONSULTATION. He had become so ill, he was living with his mother so she could help take care of him. He was totally jaundiced from liver damage and had been to various doctors over a long period of time. The diagnosis was obvious—severe, acute *Candida albicans*. X-rays showed spots on the lungs, which were also diagnosed as *Candida*.

The man was so desperate to be well and get back to work, he did everything his doctors told him. He had changed his diet and had superb eating habits, refusing to eat anything with sugar, fruit, yeast, etc. However, he was never given any recommendations for a probiotic or herbal combination that would attack the yeast.

During the consultation, I predicted he

would experience a turnaround within 2-4 weeks if he would follow my suggestions. He was quite negative because of his past experiences. I explained to him that having a yeast-free, sugar-free diet was a great start, but it was not enough. A good diet would not replace the good flora in his intestinal tract. We had to get something in him that would attack the *Candida* as well as replace the good flora in the intestinal tract.

Having spent all his savings and more on doctors' bills, he was very leery. I assured him we could get him on the right tract for under $100. Although very skeptical, he was so desperate he decided to give it a try.

Step #1: a daily herbal combination (anti-fungal as well as antibacterial) to attack the yeastlike fungus that had invaded his body. Step #2: a good probiotic that puts the good bacteria back into the digestive tract as well as the intestines. This good bacteria is a vital part of your immune system, digestion, and total bowel health.

His particular case was so severe that I chose not to recommend the highest potency probiotic for fear he would go into a severe healing crisis. He started with one pill, every other day! For the first two weeks he saw only marginal improvement, as we were building a foundation to work on. After two weeks, he increased to a daily dose probiotic. From that point on he improved exponentially.

Next, we attacked one of the side effects left by the yeast, a skin rash, using a hydrogen-peroxide gel. Bad bacteria cannot live in an oxygenated cell, and the rashes began to clear within a few days. At the end of sixty days, his skin was no longer jaundiced, which meant his liver function was normalizing. His energy was also returning, and best of all, hope had sprung forth again!

He recently came in for his supplements and wanted to show me his renewed skin color. It was beautifully normal, no longer yellow. He was working full-time again and feeling better than he had felt in three years!

If this sounds easy, it is—if you are willing to do your part, such as eating the right things and staying away from the foods you know are feeding the yeast. Supplement a good eating program with the things that will assist your healing. Help is on the way!

CASE #2

A precious friend called one weekend and said she was so dizzy she was vomiting profusely every time she moved. Her equilibrium was so bad that the room was spinning, and her husband was taking her to the emergency room. You should know that this dear lady is a heart transplant patient. Although she is doing well physically and runs circles around the majority of people, she has been on more medications than you could ever imagine in connection with the transplant and other associated conditions.

After various tests, the ER doctor said she had white spots on her brain, which were affecting her neurological function and causing the dizziness. But he assured her that this was quite common with people of her age and there was nothing to worry about.

Nonsense! Those white spots were *Candida*, which shows up in a white mucous in the stools as well as x-rays. Just because it is seen a lot does not mean it is something to accept as normal. It stands to reason that it shows up more as we age because the older we are, the more we tend to abuse our bodies with a bad diet and lack of exercise.

I recommended a probiotic, and she responded immediately! No problems, no side effects. She has mentioned that her sugar cravings in the evening have dissipated. She used to feel she had to bake something sweet every evening just to satisfy her sweet tooth. Now she knows the *Candida* was persuading her into baking to feed its cravings!

CASE #3

Another client, a perfectly healthy-looking thirty-two-year-old mother of three young children, whose list of ailments ranged from micro-valve prolapse to diabetes to severe sugar cravings, had been to a variety of doctors over the span of a few years. With all the diagnoses, she received quite a rich mixture of opinions as to the cause of her many complaints. I had my suspicions as well, but I knew that a total diagnostic workup was in order. I referred her to an M.D. friend of mine for this. After he had examined her, we conferred and felt she needed to go directly to a cardiologist!

The highly respected heart specialist she

visited said she needed open-heart surgery as soon as possible, or she would probably not live another year! Which, as one would expect, terrified this young mother.

We met to go over the specialist's findings, and she asked my opinion. After we prayed for God's wisdom, I told her I believed the best thing to do was to get a second opinion.

Despite the gravity of her condition, my initial suspicion was that she was eaten up with *Candida*. Her sugar cravings were overwhelming, even though she followed a healthy diet most of the time. She wouldn't even keep sugar products in the house so as not to be tempted. But when the cravings got to a certain level, she would drive to the convenience store for the sole purpose of getting a sugar fix. That's what *Candida* does—it will drive you, like a junkie to drugs, or an alcoholic to liquor.

I suggested she call another cardiologist who came with great references and was not interested in operating without investigating every possible alternative first. Amazingly, and unknown to me, this doctor had just finished a study on the role of *Candida* as a cause of micro-valve prolapse. Such is the grace of our God!

And just as I suspected, she was one of these cases. No surgery was needed, but a tactical plan was established to clean up her inner terrain from the horrid yeastlike fungus that was literally taking over her very life.

With the correct diagnosis, a wonderful peace came over this young mother of three. Then a regimen of cleansing and nutritional supplementation was put in place to restore what had been stolen from her health. As she began this process, energy, vitality, and healing began to flow back into her body.

CASE #4

One of my first experiences with severe *Candida* was back in the 1980s. A businessman who worked twelve-hour days with no apparent health problems would lie down at night and begin to experience severe breathing problems. His M.D. didn't find anything abnormal, and there were no other symptoms. Today he would have most likely been diagnosed with panic attacks, but in the early '80s they just admitted that they did not know what caused that type of condition.

On several occasions the situation was so

bad that his wife had to call 911. Although rushed to the hospital three different times, they weren't able to diagnose him. Finally he'd had enough. He sought out alternative professional advice to get to the root of his phantom physical dilemma.

The alternative physician made a rapid diagnosis—*Candida*. Many years before the onset of this symptom, the patient had a severe drinking problem. The yeast in the alcohol set him up with major *Candida albicans*. Over the years he had minor troubles with allergies, digestive problems, chemical sensitivity, as well as being slightly overweight. Different physicians had treated all of these symptoms individually.

When he started on the *Candida* cleanse, the breathing attacks in the evening ceased *immediately*. The allergies left, as did the chemical sensitivity and the digestive problems, and he took off thirty pounds. Not only did he look ten years younger, but he felt and acted like it as well. The human body has wonderful healing potential if we'll only give it a chance.

LEAKY GUT SYNDROME

AS NOTED PREVIOUSLY, *CANDIDA* OVERGROWTH CAN CAUSE MANY DISORDERS to develop, but one of the more severe disorders is called Leaky Gut Syndrome. It occurs after a long-term infestation when the *Candida* shifts into a fungal form and develops long rootlike structures (rhizoids) that penetrate into the intestinal wall, creating microscopic breaks in the normal mucosal boundary of the gastrointestinal tract. The resulting miniscule pinholes cause the intestine to become porous, allowing foreign substances and toxins and undigested proteins and carbohydrates to leak directly into the bloodstream, which in turn creates antibodies (proteins) to attack these as if they were foreign germs, resulting in inflammation.

Leaky Gut Syndrome describes an intestinal permeability and is a common but poorly recognized problem. Millions of people have inflammatory bowel disease, over one million

Americans suffer from Crohn's disease, and another 500,000 have ulcerative colitis. All of these conditions occur when different areas of the intestinal tract become irritated and inflamed. While they are different diseases, they share a common problem—leaky gut.

The symptoms are wide-ranging and include:

- food allergies
- interference with hormonal activity
- mood swings
- depression
- joint and connective tissue pain and inflammation
- psoriasis
- eczema
- irritable bowel syndrome
- fatigue
- anemia

Combine this syndrome with stress, a poor diet, and lack of exercise, and you create a favorable environment for more *Candida* overgrowth and parasites. With a weakened immune system and impaired digestion, the body lacks the proper amounts of digestive enzymes, such as pepsin, and digestive agents, such as hydrochloric acid, both of which help to kill parasites. Patients with *Candida* usually have parasites, whether microscopic or hookworms, roundworms, and pinworms. Parasites coexist well with yeast and find the body's digestive system a warm home to prosper in.

Untreated, the continued entrance of leaking toxins into the bloodstream causes additional chemical sensitivities such as allergies and environmental illness (reactions to carpet odors and household detergents, for instance). With an immune system confused between its own proteins and foreign proteins, food allergies become rampant. And since 60 percent of our antibodies are produced in the intestinal tract, the body's immunity is compromised in many ways.

STEPS TO HEALING

Please go back and reread the previous section on "Treatment of *Candida Albicans*." It is absolutely imperative that you take the right steps to remove any of the pathogenic organisms from your system, including the *Candida*. In particular, we have developed a powerful new natural agent called the *Candida Cleanse*. It is specifically formulated for total *Candida* cleansing and works with our other new product, the *Para Cleanse*, to rid the body of parasites.

You must then go on to change your diet to one that will not encourage the growth of *Candida* as well as to re-inoculate your body with proper nutrition, particularly the intestinal microflora and agents that support your immunological functions. You need to repair the mucosal lining of your intestinal wall and heal the leaky gut. Make note of the herbs, the importance of water, and probiotics that were discussed in the "Treatment" section.

Keep in mind that the small intestine is approximately 20 feet long and lined with millions of tiny villi that are fingerlike projections that have the primary responsibility for the absorption of nutrients. If you flatten out the villi and the small intestinal wall, it would stretch as wide as a tennis court. It is an enormous surface dedicated to the absorption of approximately 90 percent of the nutrients for your body. Digested food and fiber make up about 60 percent of the mass that travels through the intestinal tract. The rest of the volume is made up of mucous and bacteria. Restabilizing the friendly bacteria has everything to do with your future health.

The good news is that the lining of the small bowel is the fastest-growing tissue of the body, changing every three days. With the proper treatment, you can experience significant healing in a week or two. Complete healing could take up to months, depending upon your health and whether you stick with the proper diet program.

DETOXIFICATION

DETOXIFICATION IS A CLEANSING
PROCESS THAT IS GOING ON INSIDE
YOUR BODY every second of your life. If
your body fails to eliminate its toxins daily,
eventually you will die an earlier death than
you should have. Our purpose here is to
explore ways you can help this process that
is so essential to rejuvenating the body and
keeping Candida and other yeast conditions
dead in their tracks. You can improve the
quality of your life as well as the length of
your life by following the suggestions I set
forth in this chapter.

Fasting is one method of detoxification to
which I devoted an entire chapter in my book,
How to Feel Great All the Time. I consider it
the most effective and practical and quickest
way to cleanse your system. Yet I recognize
that it is a more extreme form. There are
many ways to detoxify, some of which we will
consider in this chapter.

No one escapes toxins in this world. A toxin describes the chemicals in your body that have not been "detoxed" (made harmless). Toxicity occurs on two primary levels. First, toxins are taken in from our environment through the air we breathe, the food and water we consume, and through physical contact with them—environmental pollutants, food additives, and chemicals being the major ones. The majority of allergens and drugs and also mercury fillings in the teeth can create toxic elements in the body.

Second, your body produces toxins naturally all the time. Biochemical, cellular, and bodily activities generate waste substances that need to be eliminated. Free radicals, for instance, are biochemical toxins. When these are not removed, they can cause tissues and cells to become irritated or inflamed, blocking normal functions on a cellular, organ, and whole-body level. Yeasts, intestinal bacteria, foreign bacteria, and parasites produce metabolic waste products that we must process and eliminate from our bodies. Even stress creates a toxic state, if we allow it to dominate our mind and emotions for extended periods of time.

Your body was designed by God to eliminate toxins, but over time these chemicals can build up in your system and overwhelm your ability to remove them. Or you yourself might be overpowering your system by the amount of toxins you are taking in physically, emotionally, or spiritually. Some drugs and many pesticides produce immediate, dramatic toxic symptoms. Others take a long time to develop into a manifest disease, such as asbestos exposure that invisibly leads to lung cancer. It is no surprise that toxicity diseases such as cardiovascular disease and cancer have increased as our world has become more toxic. Many skin problems, allergies, arthritis, and obesity are others. In addition, a wide range of less frightening symptoms, such as headaches, fatigue, pains, coughs, constipation, gastrointestinal problems, and problems from immune weakness, can all be related to toxicity.

YOUR BODY IS A TOTAL SYSTEM

You were given five central systems that work together moment by moment to eliminate toxins. It is your responsibility to maintain their health. These systems include the *respiratory*—lungs, bronchial tubes, throat, sinuses, and nose; *gastrointestinal*—liver, gallbladder, colon, and whole GI tract; *urinary*—kidneys, bladder, and urethra; *skin and dermal*—sweat and sebaceous glands and tears; and *lymphatic*—lymph channels and lymph nodes.

The liver filters out foreign substances and wastes from the blood, metabolically altering the toxins and making them easier for the organs to eliminate and less harmful to the body. It also dumps wastes through the bile into the intestines, where much waste is eliminated. The kidneys filter wastes from the blood into the urine, while the lungs remove volatile gases as we breathe. We also get rid of heavy metals through sweating. Our sinuses and skin may also be accessory elimination organs whereby excess mucus or toxins can be released, as with sinus congestion or skin rashes.

A detoxification program is designed to safely and gently enhance your body's own natural processes. It can be done at several levels and refers to many different programs that cleanse the body of toxins. Anything that promotes elimination can be said to help us detoxify. Drinking more water will usually help you eliminate more toxins. Eating more fruits and vegetables—the high-water-content, cleansing foods—and less meat and dairy products creates less congestion and more elimination. Some programs are directed toward specific organs, such as the liver or kidneys or skin. The secret to great health and feeling great is to combine these detoxification programs into a lifestyle program that works for you.

WHAT ARE YOU EATING?

Step #1—*start eating right.* If you cut your toxic intake, you cut your need for cleansing. If you don't correct a bad diet, you drastically reduce the effectiveness of any other cleansing methods you use. In my book, *How to Feel Great All the Time*, I provide my preference in detoxification diets, which is called the Levitical Diet. I favor it because it is well balanced and proven to have been effective for thousands of years.

Detoxification diets help the body eliminate toxins in many ways. They generally eliminate the foods that commonly trigger problems with digestion and elimination. My favorite diet is about 70 percent fruits, vegetables, nuts, and grains; 25 percent cold-water fish and hormone-free chicken; and about 3-5 percent hormone-free red meat. Whatever diet you choose, *it must be balanced.* If you have any questions regarding your diet, consult a professional nutritionist, Naturopath, or physician.

FROM START TO FINISH

While it's a subject most of us prefer not to discuss, cleansing the bowels consistently is a vital key to good health. Your bowels should move like a newborn's, many times a day. One movement now and then is dangerous, but that can be changed. When the bowels slow down, the bad news begins. First, there is an increase of bad bacteria in the small intestine and putrefaction in the large intestine. The battle ensues when the bad bacteria weaken your immune system (which is located in the small intestine) and can result in digestive complications. When only partly digested proteins and bacterial toxins cross the intestinal wall, they can cause allergies.

Untreated, it gets ugly. The walls of the bowels become weak and deformed, as with diverticulitis, and hard crusts cover the intestinal walls and restrict movement within the bowels. In severe cases, the products of putrefaction cross the weakened walls of the large intestine and enter the bloodstream. The whole body may become poisoned, and it is possible to seriously damage your body. Enemas and colonics may be needed to break up and cleanse the bowel encrustations.

The easiest way to correct these intestinal problems is a diet of predominately raw foods. A high-quality fiber diet of fresh fruits and vegetables gets the bowels moving and strengthens the bowel walls. You may want to add extra fiber by drinking a glass of water (juice) with psyllium husk powder or another herbal laxative or 1/2 cup of oat bran daily to speed up the process.

DON'T FORGET THE SKIN

The skin is the largest organ and one of our best eliminative organs of our body. Skin cleansing is therefore a vital part of the detoxification process, particularly when it comes to the heavy metals (aluminum and mercury) that are eliminated through the skin's pores when we sweat. Consistent exercise, steam rooms, and sauna baths are excellent ways to remove toxins from the skin and maximize your health.

Basic skin care is a daily matter, beginning with using natural soaps when you bathe. Skin care products made from chemicals may be cheaper, but remember that those chemicals *will* be absorbed into the bloodstream. Though the amount may be small, it is the cumulative effect of the chemicals that damages your health over the long run. Especially stay away from sodium laurel sulfate—a known carcinogen.

Dry skin brushing is easy to do and helps in removing the outer dead skin layers and keeps the pores open. Another good technique for cleansing the skin is to towel off roughly until the skin gets slightly red. It will only take you a few minutes more than usual. Food grade hydrogen peroxide baths are excellent for energy and detoxifying. Epsom salts baths are also very good.

Herbal Power

Detoxification diets are the primary means to cleansing your system, and herbs have been used medicinally for centuries to supplement the cleansing of the blood and tissues or strengthening the function of specific organs. Many herbs have been proven as powerful neutraceutical agents that can support or even cause detoxification. There are hundreds of possible medicinal herbs, and they also provide vitamins, minerals, and enzymes for excellent nutrition. I have a large section on herbs in the "Nature's Prescriptions for Feeling Great" in my book, *How to Feel Great All the Time*. It includes a chart showing herbal alternatives to drugs, essential medicinal herbs, and specific concerns about herbs.

Many people utilize an herbal cleanse. For example, first thing in the morning they may drink a glass of steam-distilled water with a teaspoon of blackstrap molasses and a teaspoon of apple cider vinegar added. During the morning they drink a glass of water with psyllium husk powder, which they follow with a second glass of water. During their meals they take digestive enzymes. Between meals they may take liver herbs and drink herbal teas that specifically help support the liver.

The Fight Against Free Radicals

In the process of metabolism or oxidation, our body cells produce molecules called free radicals. They are unstable molecules that attempt to steal electrons from any available source, such as our body tissues. Antioxidants, such as beta-carotene, Vitamins A, E, and especially C, and selenium, work to neutralize these unstable chemicals and protect us from them. Vitamin C is very essential to any detoxification programs because the body uses it for energy to process and eliminate these toxic wastes. The more antioxidants we get in our diets, the more we are able to stop these damaging effects. The main source of antioxidants is fruits, vegetables, nuts, grains, and cold-pressed plant oils.

Antioxidants are essential for detoxification because they help cells neutralize free radicals that can cause mutations and cellular damage. This damage is partly responsible for a wide range of illnesses, including all the degenerative diseases such as arthritis, cardiovascular disease, Alzheimer's, and cancer. Any shortage of antioxidants can become catastrophic to one's health. When our antioxidants are low, energy is not available and detoxification cannot take place in a normal fashion. Therefore, toxins accumulate or are stored until they can be processed and eliminated.

Other excellent sources of antioxidants are found in bioflavonoids, grape seed extract, ginseng, garlic, molybdenum, DHEA, wheat and barley grass, Echinacea, manganese, carotenoids, Ginkgo Biloba, melatonin, L-Cysteine, acetyl-l-carnite, CoQ10, milk thistle, and B-vitamins.

YOU ARE WHAT YOU ABSORB

Enzymes have a major impact on your health and detoxification. They help digest and absorb proteins, carbohydrates or starches, lipids or fats. Absorption is absolutely crucial to your health. They also clean up dead tissues, enhance your own enzyme capacity, and help the bowels in cleansing, because they liquefy the bowel content and make for a quicker passage.

The best source of enzymes is fresh raw fruits and vegetables, which can be supplemented with multidigestive enzymes. Unfortunately, enzymes are destroyed by processing and cooking. If you eat a high proportion of processed foods, you lose out on these vital ingredients. By eating a wide range of foods, as close to their raw state as possible, you can enjoy all these benefits.

CONCLUSION

If left untreated, *Candida albicans* can become a dangerous infection that will spread and weaken the body's immune system to fight off disease. Because I believe in the body's amazing ability to heal itself when we follow the guidelines God has given us, I strongly suggest using this natural approach to remove this yeastlike fungus from your body. By eliminating the overgrowth from your system, it will primarily decrease the stress from your immune system.

There may be some cases that are so severe they require special treatment from a licensed health care professional. There are certain pharmaceutical drugs that have been used by some to treat severe cases of *Candida*. Please consult a medical doctor if the need arises.

VALERIE SAXION'S SILVER CREEK LABS

IN THIS BOOKLET, I HAVE NOTED ONE OF OUR PRODUCTS, the *Candida Cleanse*, that will help you stop *Candida* and other yeast conditions dead in their tracks. I also recommend that you consider three of our other products that will promote a healthy body that is able to prevent future problems. To order these products or to contact Silver Creek Laboratories for a complete catalog and order form of other nutritional supplements and health products, call (817) 236-8557, toll free at (800) 493-1146, fax (817) 236-5411, or write us at:

9555 Harmon Road
Fort Worth, TX 76177.

Body Oxygen. A pleasant-tasting nutritional supplement that is meticulously manufactured with cold pressed aloe vera. The aloe is used as a stabilized carrier for numerous nutritional constituents, including magnesium peroxide and pure anaerocidal oxygen, hawthorne berry, ginkgo biloba, ginseng, and St. John's Wort. It helps naturally fight infections, inflammation, and degeneration by taking oxygen in at the cellular level. It also commonly helps in colon cleansing, regular elimination, and provides a feeling of increased energy and mental alertness.

Candida Cleanse. A decade in coming, this is the most powerful natural agent I know of in the fight against *Candida*. It is specifically formulated for TOTAL *Candida* cleansing. A two-part system is also available to rid the body of *Candida* and parasites called the Para Cleanse.

Dr. Lorenzen's Clustered Water is probably the greatest breakthrough in health science product development in this century. Clustered Water, produced at home using one ounce of solution to one gallon of steam-distilled water, replenishes the most vital support for all cellular DNA and the 4,000 plus enzymes that are involved in every metabolic process in your body. This amazing product increases nutrient absorption by up to 600 percent, which means your vitamins and organic foods will deliver far more vital nutrients to your body. It replicates the powerful healing waters of the earth! Excellent for cleaning out lymphatic fluids! It comes in a C-400 formula for those who are generally healthy and detoxed, and a SBX formula for the immune-compromised.

Creation's Bounty. Simply the best, pleasant-tasting, green, whole, raw, organic food supplement available—a blend of whole, raw, organic herbs and grains, principally amaranth, brown rice, spirulina, and flaxseed. This combination of live foods with live enzymes assists your body in the digestion of foods void of enzymes. You will gain vital nutrients, protein, carbohydrates, and good fats to nourish your body and brain, resulting in extra energy and an immunity boost as well. It is a whole food, setting it apart from other green foods on the market.

ParaCease is a natural herbal supplement formulated to help rid the body of unwanted Candida and parasites. ParaCease contains 16 powerful natural compounds with anti-fungal and anti-parasitic properties. These herbs, minerals, and fatty acids have long been used to assist the body in maintaining internal health. A cleanse program with ParaCease combined with sensible diet changes will leave you feeling energized, rejuvenated, and healthy.

Unleash Your Greatness

AT BRONZE BOW PUBLISHING WE ARE COMMITTED

to helping you achieve your ultimate potential

in functional athletic strength, fitness, natural

muscular development, and all-around superb

health and youthfulness.

Our books, videos, newsletters, Web sites, and training seminars will bring you the very latest in scientifically validated information that has been carefully extracted and compiled from leading scientific, medical, health, nutritional, and fitness journals worldwide.

Our goal is to empower you! To arm you with the best possible knowledge in all facets of strength and personal development so that you can make the right choices that are appropriate for *you*.

Now, as always, **the difference between greatness and mediocrity** begins with a choice. It is said that knowledge is power. But that statement is a half truth. Knowledge is power only when it has been tested, proven, and applied to your life. At that point knowledge becomes wisdom, and in wisdom there truly is *power*. The power to help you choose wisely.

So join us as we bring you the finest in health-building information and natural strength training strategies to help you reach your ultimate potential.

FOR INFORMATION ON ALL OUR EXCITING NEW SPORTS AND FITNESS PRODUCTS, CONTAC

BRONZE BOW PUBLISHING
2600 East 26th Street
Minneapolis, MN 55406

WEB SITES
www.bronzebowpublishing.co
www.masterlevelfitness.com

612.724.8200   Toll Free **866.724.8200**   FAX **612.724.899**